MW01045432

ENJOY ENTERTAINING

Children

··WITH··

THEME DAYS

More than Two Dozen
Ideas for Possible Themes

Barbara Wilson-Battiss

ENJOY ENTERTAINING CHILDREN WITH THEME DAYS

iUniverse books may be ordered through booksellers or by contacting:

iUniverse
1663 Liberty Drive
Bloomington, IN 47403
www.iuniverse.com
1-800-Authors (1-800-288-4677)

ISBN: 978-1-5320-4508-0 (sc)
ISBN: 978-1-5320-4507-3 (e)

Library of Congress Control Number: 2018904205

Print information available on the last page.

iUniverse rev. date: 04/17/2018

Introduction

Fun, laughter, and learning is guaranteed. Elementary school children will love the time you share with them. However, the leader must get prepared ahead of time by either visiting a library or getting information online at home. Many DOLLAR STORES (DS) and THRIFT SHOPS (TS) are invaluable as they stock inexpensive items that can be used. These should be visited to get many ideas and objects like books for your theme.

A Theme Day can be once a week/month or one summer week. The themes could also be used for birthday party ideas.

Decide the hours to be covered such as 9:00-1:00; 12:00-5:00; or 9:00-4:00. These themes include lunch ideas, physical activity, snacks and some game ideas. Feel free to add any of your thoughts and ideas to the day.

Please note that I have actually used many of these themes with my own grandchildren and everyone enjoyed the experience. Ten years later they still mention these times with visiting cousins and friends.

I dedicate this book to my 4 grandchildren...

To Ashleigh and Tyler who participated in most of the themes

And to Liam and Ryan for all the crafts like gingerbread houses and tree ornaments that we shared....

May God bless the 4 of you always....

Grandma

Contents

Travel

In all trips it adds extra fun if you use a dining room table or kitchen as part of an airline and you act as a flight attendant. A hat and scarf is all that is required. Use a belt for seat belt and have a small activity to do as well as a small drink. Fifteen minutes is plenty and then announce the arrival to the country.

Also if you can photo some money of that country for each to buy souvenirs or pay for lunch! Small souvenirs can be found at DS or TS which they buy at the end of their trip. A hot country could use a hat etc.

HAWAII

ACTIVITY

-Draw or use a flag of the country and any info etc

-Bake Macadamia nut cookies

-Glue popsicle sticks to a can and paint it like a beach

-Make leis from flowers or add flowers to small plastic leis

- Make a beach inside of a shoe box on its side. Cut the top and paint a blue sky and darker blue water on the back. Spread and glue sand to the bottom and place the umbrellas and shells.

LUNCH	-Oriental foods or chicken rice soup
	-Pineapple up-side-down cake
	-Use pineapple shaped glasses from DS for drink
EXERCISE	-Swim or climb Diamond Head (Volcano) by using stairs (x2 or 3
SNACK	-The macadamia nut cookie
MATERIALS LIST	-Picture of Hawaiin flag and information on Hawaii (on line)
	-Macadamia nut cookie ingredients
	-Popsicle sticks (DS)
	-Glue (DS)
	-Assorted paints (DS)
	-flowers for leis (DS)
	-Small plastic leis (optional) (DS)
	-shoe box for each child
	-Blue and white paint (lighten the blue for sky (DS)
	-Shells (DS)
	-Umbrellas for drinks (DS)
	-Plastic pineapple shaped glasses (DS)
	-FOOD: Oriental food or soup, Frozen pineapple cake

TIP

-Any bright t-shirt that the children own would look good

-For ready made macadamia cookies see Subway store

-For souvenirs: scarves,pearls,gold charms & bracelets, flip-flops (DS or TS or your own)

Travel (2)

ITALY

ACTIVITY

-A map of Italy and their flag
-mention site to see and show pictures
-what do they make and export: cars, wine, furniture, clothing
-Most Italian games are played outdoors: Strega (Witch) requires 3 or more to play: Witch calls out a colour and the others must touch something of that colour before the witch can touch one of them; the touched one becomes the next witch
-game: Regina (Queen) faces the others a distance away. They ask her How many steps to you? She answers with a number and an animal. They must take the no. of steps and act like that animal. The first to reach the queen wins.

LUNCH

-Pasta
-Gelato (Ice Cream) for dessert
-Wash a Chianti or wine bottle out and fill with red punch; serve in small wine glasses (preferably plastic)

EXERCISE	Soccer game or ride across pool on a float to the other side (race?) like a gondola ride or water taxi
SNACK	-Fruit like mango, peach and grapes
MATERIALS LIST	-Map of Italy and flag -Any pictures of Italy (Library or on line) -Soccer ball or floating item for pool (DS) -Used Chianti or wine bottle -Wine glasses (DS) -FOOD: Pasta, ice cream, peach, grapes or mango
TIP	-They could buy souvenirs before returning home on the airplane: Samples: leather change purse, ceramics, stationery, shoes (DS or TS or your own)

Travel (3)

AFRICA

ACTIVITY

-Colour any colouring or activity book with African items (DS
-Create a picture with stickers (DS) and colour
-AMPE game with all children standing apart and all jump when the Ampe says so with one leg out front. Those with the same leg as Ampe get one point and the winner is the first to get 10 points.
-KUPOBA game with all the marbles in a wooden (unbreakable) bowl, each child, one at a time, throws one marble up in the air, then try to get the most marbles out from the bowl and catch the first marble before it lands back in the bowl. The most marbles wins.
-Play African Bingo (see tip below)

LUNCH

-picnic lunch on blanket on grass or floor: Only a spoon and bowl.
-In the middle have a salad, cold cuts, olives etc
-fruit salad for dessert
-Drink in a jar or can

<u>EXERCISE</u>	-Take a safari using the stuffed animals available and walk for 15 min.
<u>SNACK</u>	-Berries
<u>MATERIALS LIST</u>	-Colouring/Activity book with African items per child (DS) -Stickers of Africa (DS) -Marbles (DS) -Wooden bowl or unbreakable one (DS or TS) -Design Bingo cards -Jars or clean can per child -FOOD: salad, cold cuts, olives, fruit cups, berries
<u>TIP</u>	-African Bingo: Draw up a blank card with 5 columns and rows with an X in the middle. Each column has some item using these headings: Countries, Animals, Places like waterfalls, People, Special Famous items(see on line for breakdown) Mix each card. -Possible souvenirs: wooden items and animals, diamonds (DS or TS or your own).

Travel (4)

MEXICO

ACTIVITY
-Bean race; carry a bean on a spoon to a distant place
-Telephone game: whisper a message to each other and see what the last person hears
-Dominoes
-Make Mexican Wedding cookies (See online)
-Draw the Mexican flag
-Jump rope

LUNCH
-Tacos or Fajitas
-Fruit cup for dessert
-Ice Tea

EXERCISE
-Sombrero Dance or Climb stairs like an Aztec mountain

SNACK   -Mexican Wedding cookies

MATERIALS LIST -Beans
                -Spoons
                -Dominoes (DS)
                -Mexican Wedding cookie ingredients
                -Picture of Mexican flag (On line)
                -Skipping rope (DS)
                -Sombrero hat per child (DS)
                -Pinata (homemade or bought at DS)
                -Trinkets or candy for pinata (DS) if
                needed
                -FOODS: Tacos or fajitas, fruit cups, Ice
                tea drink

TIP   -End with a piñata of candy or trinkets
                -Wear bright clothes and sombrero hats
                if possible
                -Souvenirs: silver, chocolate, Mayan masks,
                pottery, clothes (DS or TS or your own)

Shapes

ROUND

ACTIVITY

-How many coins in a jar? Use nickels or dimes
Could be the number of coins or the total value of jar to win
-Games like Kerplunk or any with round pieces
-Draw faces on round balloons with markers
-Use sequins in a picture that was coloured and frame it
-Use marbles in a Chinese checkers board or against a wall
-Jacks with a round small ball
-Story about a round item (DS or Library)

LUNCH

-Small pizza each or a large one
-a pie or round cookies for dessert
-drink in a round glass

EXERCISE

-Any sport with a round ball

<u>SNACK</u>	-Smarties or M&Ms

<u>MATERIALS LIST</u>
-Jar of coins
-Games with round pieces
-Round balloons (DS)
-Assorted markers
-Sequins (DS)
-Frames (optional) (DS or TS)
-Marbles (DS)
-Game of Jacks
-Round ball for exercise (DS or TS)
-FOOD: pizza, pie or cookies, Smarties or M&Ms

<u>TIP</u>
-Other shapes could be used such as square, rectangle etc
-Heart shape could use many items from Valentine's Day
-Oval could use Easter eggs etc

Colours

GREEN

Everyone wears a green top. Many green items can be used from St. Patrick's Day (DS)

ACTIVITY -Find board games with a green background such as a Snakes & Ladders like the one I found at the DS. I used gummy worms like snakes and they got to eat one every time they had to go down a snake which saved unhappy or angry moments and we laughed every time.
-Use colouring books and paint books with a lot of scenery in it.
-Plant some seeds in a green pot with earth.
-Stickers on a green paper or green stickers on white paper to tell a story.

LUNCH -Green Salad of greens, cucumber with skin attached, celery, green pepper strips, and green string beans
-green gelatin
-green glasses from St. Patrick's Day with milk or drink

<u>EXERCISE</u>	-Fill green balloons with water and toss to each other -Green ball for soccer
<u>SNACK</u>	-Green apple or green grapes, or kiwi
<u>MATERIALS LIST</u>	-Green board game (DS) -Colouring/paint books for each child (DS) -Seeds, earth and green pots (DS) -Green stickers (floral and trees?) (DS) -Green balloons or green soccer ball for exercise (DS) -FOOD: green salad items, green gelatin, green apples or grapes or kiwi
<u>TIP:</u>	Other colours like RED, BLUE, WHITE, BLACK, YELLOW etc can be used. Also could combine 2 colours for the day.

Animals

TEDDY BEAR

Collect all teddy bears in your home and bring them to the room.

Look up information on teddy bears and their name. (Library or Online)

ACTIVITY	-Colour or have activity books with bears such as Pooh
	-Story with Pooh
	-Teach the bears like a teacher
LUNCH	-On a blanket (picnic style) with all the bears have
	-chicken nuggets with honey
	-Berries for dessert
	-drink in wide glass
EXERCISE	-Sing "Teddy Bears Picnic" and dance with bears

SNACK   Gummy bears or bear shaped cookies

MATERIALS LIST -Teddy bears
                -Activity/colouring books with bears for
                each child (DS)
                -Pooh book or story (library or on line)
                -Words to 'Teddy Bears Picnic' song (on
                line)
                -FOOD: chicken nuggets, honey, berries,
                bear shaped cookies or gummy bear candy

TIP   Some shopping centers have a "Make a
                Bear" store.

Animals (2)

PENGUINS

Look up information on penguins at Library or online. Penguin Day is Apr. 25

Everyone wears white and black clothes.

ACTIVITY   -Show a map of the Southern hemisphere and point out where the penguins live. (On line for the information)
-Find stories and pictures of black/white places/people etc
-Mix up letters to words that involve penguins such as cold, snow, fish, water, swim, fins etc
-any game on white/black boards
-games like checkers board and use only the black checkers with white buttons instead of red to represent the colours of penguins

LUNCH   -Shrimp and dip or fish sticks
-Ice cream or chocolate sundae
-Milk, white or chocolate

EXERCISE   Swim

<u>SNACK</u>	-Oreo cookies
<u>MATERIALS LIST</u>	-Map of the world south of the equator -List of scrambled words that involve penguins -Checker board or any with black/white background (DS) -FOOD: shrimp or fish sticks, ice cream,chocolate syrup (optional) Oreo cookies or any with similar colouring
<u>TIP</u>	-Dollar Store might have a fish game to play in the pool. -Place a floating piece in the pool and throw a small white or black item to it ten times and count how successful each person is.

Animals (3)

CATS & DOGS

ACTIVITY
-Activity and colouring books with dogs and cats
-Bake cookies in the shape of dog bones and decorate
-List dog names and cat ones and scramble them
-List dog and cat names to see who can get the most
-Use wool in some way such as make a ball the fastest

LUNCH
-Use a new dog/cat dish with stew or chili
-Cookies from above
-milk

EXERCISE
Run race or tag game

SNACK   -chocolate raisins

MATERIALS LIST   -Activity/Colouring books of cats/dogs
                         for each child (DS)
                         -Cookie ingredients
                         -Ball of wool per child (DS)
                         -Dog or cat dish per child (DS)
                         FOOD: Stew or chili, chocolate raisins

TIP   Check the animal toys at the DS for a gift
                         of a new dog or cat for each child

Sports

OLYMPICS

As all sports are enjoyed during the Olympics, a day devoted to sports is enjoyed by all.

ACTIVITY
-Paint a flag or country name on a white t-shirt or hat to wear later
-Watch a sport on tv for a short while. Pick the last 1/2 hour so that you get the final win.
-Colour a colouring book with sport pictures
-Dollar Store has a lot of sport games and puzzles

LUNCH
-Any foreign lunch such as a meat sandwich from European countries like salami
-Any dessert from another country such as tiramisu or gelato (ice Cream)
-Milk

EXERCISE
-Play any sport like soccer, basketball, etc that is played in the Olympics
Swim, dive, or skate (Winter)

SNACK   -a foreign chocolate bar or candy

MATERIALS LIST -White T-Shirt or hat or any other item
to paint
-Colouring book with sports for each
child (DS)
-Any sports game or puzzle (DS)
-FOOD: Meat for sandwich, ice cream
or frozen tiramisu, candy or Chocolate
bar from another country

TIP   -Tape the sport to watch for 1/2 hour
instead of picking one at random

Beach Day

ACTIVITY
-Make a small kite with paper and string to fly
-Read a story about the sea (Library)
-Use shells to make a beach scene: place a shoe box on its long side and remove the other long side, paint the background (back and sides) in blues for sky and water. Glue on the bottom and spread fine sand for beach. Add drink umbrellas and small seashells. Paint birds in sky:

LUNCH
-On a blanket outdoors or floor, a sandwich or hot dog
-Squares or cookies for dessert
- Fruit punch for drink in a carton, bottle or can

EXERCISE
-Play frisbee or toss a beach ball

SNACK   -Shell chocolates

MATERIALS LIST   -Paper and string for kite or buy one at DS per child to build
-Book with the sea, lake, etc as topic (on line or Library)
-Shells (DS)
-Shoe box per child
-Blue and white paint (for lighter blue) (DS)
-Glue (DS)
Fine sand (DS)
Umbrellas for drinks (DS)
Frisbee or beach ball (DS)
FOOD: Hot dogs, squares or cookies, shell chocolates, drinks

TIP   -Wear bathing suits or shorts and sleeveless top. Use theme beside a pool if possible

Rainbow

ACTIVITY

-Explain how rainbows are formed and their colours
-Create a rainbow with coloured sand on paper or paper plate
-Make jewelry with rainbow coloured items such as small balls etc
-Colour a picture using all the rainbow colours
-See DS for many crafts using these colours

LUNCH

-Tomato sandwich with yellow and green pepper slices or any other colourful vegetable
-Cookies with M&M or coloured candies on them for dessert
-Fruit punch or any colourful drink

EXERCISE

-Plant seeds of colourful flowers outdoors or make an artificial floral arrangement in a vase

SNACK   -Grapes, pear, peach

MATERIALS LIST -Book on information of rainbows (on
                line)
                -Coloured sand (DS)
                -Large paper plates
                -Items to make jewelry (DS)
                -Coloured crayons or markers (DS)
                -Seeds and small bright pot with earth or
                artificial flowers (DS)
                -FOODS: tomatoes, peppers in yellow,
                red, green, cookies with M&M or coloured
                candies, fruit punch, grapes, pears, or
                peaches

TIP   -Wear rainbow multi-coloured t-shirts
                that you own if possible.

Castles

ACTIVITY	-Read a book about castles and the medieval life at that time
	-Colour in colouring books with castles or old time pictures
	-Show some family pictures and tell tales about them: preferably former generations
	-Talk about how knights and moats were necessary for safety. Use cardboard amd duct tape to create swords.
	-Entertainment could be a play to perform or poetry readings: have a play or some poems ready to use. (On line or Library)
LUNCH	-Like old times use spoon or hands only:
	-Large pieces of meat (Chicken or beef), large pieces of raw vegetable like celery or carrots
	-tarts to pick up
	-cup of milk
EXERCISE	-Skip or play ball

SNACK   -cookies

MATERIALS LIST -Book on castles (library)
-Colouring book with ancient pictures (DS)
-Play or poems (On line or Library)
-Ball (DS)
-King and queen crowns (DS)
-FOOD: meat, carrots, celery, tarts, cookies

TIP   -Wear sweaters and long skirts for girls as castles are very cold
-Decide on a King and Queen; dress in Purple and have crowns

Pirates

ACTIVITY
-Use a fishing game in the bathtub
-Shell craft; glue shells to the cover of a box for jewelry etc
-Temporary tattoos
-Book or information on mermaids
-Maps with hidden treasure that you decide on and they guess: could be of your home
-Make small paper boats
-Make an eye patch from black construction paper and add elastic.

LUNCH
-Tomato soup with fish noodles in it or any soup with Golden fish crackers
-apple for dessert
-Drink in a bowl

EXERCISE
-walk the plank (sidewalk or into a pool)

<u>SNACK</u>	-Popsicle (water)
<u>MATERIALS LIST</u>	-Fishing game from DS if possible -Shells (DS) -Glue -Box or container with lid -Temporary tattoos (DS) -Book on mermaids (Library) -Map of your home for hidden treasure: one per child -Paper for boats –Black construction paper & elastic for eye patch (May be bought at DS) -FOOD: tomato soup with fish noodles, golden fish crackers, apples, popsicles
<u>TIP</u>	-An eye patch and scarf around the head will make everyone a pirate

A to Z

"B"

For an alphabet day use a dictionary & make a list of possible words such as the following:

Beans, bottle, broccoli, basket, baby, bunny, bear, book, beach, ball, bus, bead, bag, bat, bed, bell, bike, bow, boat, blanket, blouse, BBQ, barrel, butterfly, banana, blueberry.

ACTIVITY
-spin a BOTTLE to do an act (assortment in a bowl & picked by actor)
-Make a necklace with BEADS
-Decorate a BASKET with sewing decorations
-Draw a BOAT on paper

LUNCH
-On a blanket have BBQ chicken with BROCCOLI or a pig in a BLANKET (hot dog wrapped)
-BANANA or BLUEBERRIES for dessert
-BOTTLE of water or drink

EXERCISE
-Ride a BIKE or BUS or play BASKETBALL or BASEBALL

<u>SNACK</u>	-Gummy BEARS

<u>MATERIALS LIST</u>
-Bowl with acting ideas
-Empty bottle
-Beads (DS)
-Baskets and sewing decorations such as ribbon, buttons etc per child (DS or TS or your own)
-Ball for sport (DS)
-FOOD: BBQ chicken, broccoli (optional) or hot dogs, bananas, blueberries, bottle of water or drink, gummy bears

TIP
-Wear BLUE or BROWN clothes that you own

"C"

<u>ACTIVITY</u>	-How many COINS in a jar? -Bake some CUPCAKES or CHEWY COOKIES -Copy a CLOCK – CARD game; place Ace to Queen in a clock style layout with the King in the center all upside down. Do this for all cards till the last one which you turn over and place it where the time is. Then turn over the first card at that spot and continue to place all the cards till you get the 4th King. End of game. Count how many you did not uncover. The one with the least wins Several decks may be needed or each takes their turn. -Play games like CHECKERS, CHESS, or CARDS
<u>LUNCH</u>	-Grilled CHEESE sandwich with CHIPS -CUPCAKES or COOKIES for dessert -CUP of milk or hot CHOCOLATE
<u>EXERCISE</u>	-Walk to the CORNER & CHECK out how many CARS by COLOUR

SNACK	-Small CHOCOLATE bar

MATERIALS LIST	-Jar with coins: know how many coins & value
	-Cupcake or cookie recipe and ingredients
	-Play cards (DS)
	-checkers or chess (DS)
	-FOOD: grilled cheese, chips, Small chocolate bar

TIP	-Wear a COWBOY hat (DS) and eat in a circle outdoors

"S"

<u>ACTIVITY</u>	-Make a picture with SAND, SHELLS, SEEDS
	-Cut pictures from a magazine with SCISSORS
	-Name as many pieces of clothing that starts with S eg: shoe, sock, suit, slippers, skirt, shirt, scarf, sweater. If they get SIX or SEVEN they win a SUCKER
	-Put 6 items on a tray that begin with S and a cloth to hide them See how many they can remember.
	- Play SOLITAIRE and see who gets the most on the Aces
	-List people's names that start with S like Sam, Sandra
<u>LUNCH</u>	-SANDWICH or SOUP, SPAGHETTI or SALAD
	-SQUARES for dessert
	-SLUSH for drink
<u>EXERCISE</u>	-SWIM, SKATE, or play SOCCER

<u>SNACK</u>	-STRAWBERRIES
<u>MATERIALS LIST</u>	-Coloured or plain sand (DS) -Shells and Seeds (DS) -Magazine and scissors per child -Suckers (DS) -Six items that start with 'S' on a tray and covered (DS) -Playing cards (DS) -Ball for exercise (optional) -FOOD: Sandwich filling, soup, spaghetti or salad items, Strawberries
<u>TIP</u>	-Could also use any board game like Snakes & Ladders

$\mathcal{A} - \mathcal{Z}$

"T"

ACTIVITY
-Play TABLE TENNIS (if available)
-Make a TENT (Sheet over card table)
-Watch a movie or TV with a TRAIN or TRUCK ride in it
-Draw a picture of TULIPS or TREES
-Place 6 items on a TRAY that start with T and cover with a cloth. See how many are remembered
-Organize a small TRACK & FIELD day with running, jumping distance, skipping and throwing a ball for distance

LUNCH
-TOASTED TUNA or TURKEY sandwich
-TARTS for dessert
-Ice TEA in a TEAPOT

EXERCISE
-TRACK & FIELD Day: See above instructions

<u>SNACK</u>	-TANGERINE
<u>MATERIALS LIST</u>	-Card table & sheet or blanket
	-Six items that start with 'T' on a tray and covered (DS)
	-Ball and skipping rope for Track and Field
	-Teapot
	-FOOD: Tuna or Turkey, tarts. Ice tea, tangerines
<u>TIP</u>	-Wear a T-SHIRT and TROUSERS
	-For movie or tv show, choose ahead

Circus

ACTIVITY
-Juggle 2 balls
-Wear a red nose and large shoes and act like a clown
-Place several small paper plates on a table; decide a distance to throw coins and see if you can land on a plate which you keep
-Look up information about elephants
-Colour circus pictures

LUNCH
-Hot dog and chips
-Ice Cream in a cone for dessert
-Coke or other drink

EXERCISE
-Walk a straight line like a High Wire or Bicycle ride

<u>SNACK</u>	-Popcorn
<u>MATERIALS LIST</u>	-2 balls (DS)
	-Red nose (DS) per child
	-Large shoes per child (any adult's)
	-Paper plates (DS) and coins
	-Book on elephants (On line or Library)
	-Activity/colouring books with circus theme (DS)
	-FOOD: hot dogs,chips, ice cream and cones, popcorn
<u>TIP</u>	- The Dollar Store have some of the items mentioned above

Flying Objects

Please note that this theme covers all items that fly such as butterflies, bugs, airplanes, Hot-air balloons, helicopters, space ships, drones etc.

ACTIVITY

-Find books to colour or read at the DS on objects that fly

-Fill a room with balloons and see how many each can catch in a prearranged time.

-Make paper airplanes

-Make a tray of the above items and cover. Show for a few minutes and see how many thay can remember.

LUNCH

-Any meal that is flown in to your store

-Banana for dessert

-Lemonade for drink

EXERCISE

-Catch a frisbee.

<u>SNACK</u>	-Nuts (Most are flown in)
<u>MATERIALS LIST</u>	-Activity/Colouring books on the above flying objects (DS) -balloons (DS) -paper -one each of the flying objects on a tray with a cover (DS) -frisbee (DS) -FOOD: bananas, lemonade, nuts

Garden

Gardening may be done for flowers, fruit, vegetables, or plants.

ACTIVITY

-Plant some seeds outdoors or in a pot to watch grow

-Create an artificial flower in a pot or an arrangement in a vase to decorate a room

-Colour floral pictures in a colouring book

-Go to a gardening store and admire the many items

LUNCH

-Vegetable salad

-Fruit cup or fruit in gelatin cup for dessert

-Drink a fruit drink like cranberry juice

EXERCISE

-Visit a local park that has a garden or walk around your area and admire the gardens

<u>SNACK</u>	-Fresh fruit
<u>MATERIALS LIST</u>	-Seeds (DS)
	-Pot and earth (if necessary)
	-Artificial flowers (DS)
	-Colouring book with flowers per child (DS)
	-FOOD: salad items, fruit cup (with gelatin?), fruit drink, fruit
<u>TIP</u>	-Wear floral tops and green bottoms if possible

Camping

ACTIVITY

-Arts and Craft ideas from Dollar Store
-Card games
-Tug of war with long piece of cord/rope
-Fish in a tub
-Ball toss
-After lunch take a short nap in tent outdoors

LUNCH

-On a Blanket and hands only: Hot dog or Sandwich
-Bought cookies like Oreo
-Small juice carton

EXERCISE

-Swim if pool nearby; Race; Hike (climb a stairway)

SNACK   -Popsicle

MATERIALS LIST -Any arts/crafts items from DS
                        -Playing cards (DS)
                        -Long cord or rope
                        -Fishing game (DS)
                        -Ball (DS)
                        -Card table with blanket
                        -FOOD: Hot dogs, cookies, juice carton,
                        popsicles

TIP   -For tent use a blanket over a card table
                        Placed outside if possible

Numbers

ACTIVITY

-Deck of cards spread upside down on table. Each picks one card to find and keep 7s. Put back the others. One with most 7s wins.

-Colour by number

-Drop 2 dice and then turn over a card to match. (remove Kings) If no match put back for next player.

-Dominoes

-Any number game like Snakes and Ladders that uses dice

LUNCH

-Raisin Bread (count raisins: most wins)

-Grapes: eat only 10?

-Milk in a dotted glass

EXERCISE

-Hopscotch outdoors with a stone or large button

SNACK   -Chocolate chip cookies or M&M covered
                        cookies

MATERIALS LIST -Playing cards (DS)
                        -Colour by number (DS)
                        -Dice (DS)
                        -Dominoes (DS)
                        -Any game with dice (DS)
                        -FOOD: raisin bread, grapes, cookies
                        decorated with items to count like
                        M&Ms or chocolate chips

TIP   -Math questions or contests depends on
                        age of children (DS)

Farm

ACTIVITY
- List animals found on a farm
- Colour or decorate eggs
- Build a barn like a gingerbread house without windows and a double door with an upper window with straw (hay)
- Bake cookies in the shape of animals

LUNCH
- Chicken sandwich
- Carrot cake for dessert
- Milk

EXERCISE
- Use a broom stick like a horse and ride it

SNACK
- Fresh fruit or berries

MATERIALS LIST
- Eggs to decorate (kit from Easter?)
- Gingerbread house pieces as described above
- For hay..use the yellow straw for Easter baskets (DS)
- cookie ingredients and cookie animal cutters
- FOOD: chicken, carrot cake, fresh fruit or berries

TIP
- Wear jeans and plaid top if possible

Do you need more Themes? Try these suggestions....

A-Z: 22 letters not used in this book

Shapes: Square, Rectangle, Oval, Heart

Colours: Pink, Red, Blue, Purple, Yellow, Brown, White/Black

Travel: Ireland, England, Scotland, France, Spain, Belgium, Germany, Austria, China, Japan, Orient, India, Egypt, Australia, Columbia, Peru, Brazil, Costa Rica, Panama etc

About The Author

Barbara Wilson-Battiss lives with her husband Patrick in St. Catharines, Ontario Canada which is about 15 minutes from Niagara Falls. They have 2 married sons, 2 lovely daughters-in-law, and 4 grandchildren.

She is a member of Beta Sigma Phi, a world-wide organization for women. In 1992 she co-chaired the Montreal convention that attracted 503 ladies for a weekend

She also worked on the novice hockey tournament in D.D.O. a suburb of Montreal, for 20 years: 10 as registrar.

If you wish to contact her,
email her at bwilsonbattiss@cogeco.ca

Printed in the United States
By Bookmasters